W9-CAR-429

# WAR PLANES

# Night Attack Gunships:
## The AC-130H Spectres
### by Michael and Gladys Green

CAPSTONE
HIGH-INTEREST
BOOKS

an imprint of Capstone Press
Mankato, Minnesota

Capstone High-Interest Books are published by Capstone Press
151 Good Counsel Drive, P.O. Box 669, Mankato, Minnesota 56002
http://www.capstone-press.com

*Library of Congress Cataloging-in-Publication Data*
Green, Michael, 1952–
   Night attack gunships: the AC-130H Spectres/by Michael and Gladys Green.
   p. cm.—(War planes)
   Summary: Introduces the AC-130H Gunships, their specifications, weapons,
missions, and future in the Air Force.
   Includes bibliographical references and index.
   ISBN 0-7368-1509-0 (hardcover)
   1. Spectre (Gunship)—Juvenile literature. 2. Gunships (Military aircraft)—United
States—Juvenile literature. 3. Night and all-weather operations (Military aeronautics)—
United States—Juvenile literature. [1. Spectre (Gunship) 2. Gunships (Military aircraft)]
I. Green, Gladys, 1954– II. Title. III. Series.
UG1242.G85 G74 2003
623.7'464—dc21                                                          2002007925

**Editorial Credits**
Carrie Braulick, editor; Timothy Halldin, series designer; Gene Bentdahl and
   Molly Nei, book designers; Jo Miller, photo researcher

**Photo Credits**
Aero Graphics, Inc., 25
AFP/Corbis, 4
Defense Visual Information Center, cover, 1, 7, 8, 10, 16 (all), 18–19, 24 (all)
George Hall/Corbis, 22, 26
Photo by Ted Carlson/Fotodynamics, 28
Photri-Microstock, 13, 17, 20

**Special thanks to the staff of the Air Force Special Operations Command Public
Affairs Office for their help in preparing this book.**

1  2  3  4  5  6  08  07  06  05  04  03

# Table of Contents

## Chapter One

## Learn About

- Need for a gunship
- AC-130 models
- AC-130 missions

# The AC-130H in Action

A small group of U.S. soldiers is on a nighttime scouting mission in enemy territory. Enemy soldiers fire bullets at them from many directions. The U.S. troops are trapped. They use a radio to call for help.

Soon, the enemy soldiers hear a plane flying over them. It is an AC-130H Spectre gunship. The gunship's crew members fire bullets in a circle around the U.S. troops.

Seconds later, the ground near the enemy soldiers explodes. Many enemy soldiers are killed or wounded and the enemy commander orders his soldiers to retreat.

A rescue helicopter picks up the U.S. soldiers. The gunship returns to a nearby air base.

## Need for a Gunship

In the early 1960s, the U.S. military was fighting in the Vietnam War (1954–1975) in Southeast Asia. Thousands of trucks brought supplies to enemy soldiers. The supply trucks operated along jungle trails at night.

The U.S. Air Force needed a special type of plane called a gunship to destroy the supply trucks. The gunship had to travel long distances and stay in the air for long periods of time. It needed to fly slowly so pilots could see enemy trucks at night. The aircraft also had to carry weapons powerful enough to destroy large trucks.

**The Air Force first used gunships in the late 1960s.**

In 1967, Air Force pilots began to fly AC-130As.

## AC-130H Development

The Air Force made changes to planes called the AC-47 and the AC-119 to make them more capable of defeating enemy trucks. After crews flew them successfully on missions, Air Force officials decided to change a cargo plane called the C-130 into a gunship. In early 1967, manufacturers completed the first test model of the plane. Pilots flew it on its first mission against enemy trucks in late 1967. The Air Force ordered seven final models of the gunship. These gunships were called AC-130As.

The Air Force later improved its AC-130A gunships. In 1971, the Air Force started to fly the AC-130E. This gunship had larger guns and better night-vision devices than AC-130As. In 1973, manufacturers modified the AC-130E into the AC-130H. This gunship had better communications and targeting equipment. The AC-130H also had more powerful engines than earlier gunship models.

Today, the Air Force has eight AC-130Hs in service. All of these gunships are based at Hurlburt Field in Florida. AC-130H crew members provide close air support to soldiers. They also perform missions to attack targets and to protect buildings and resources.

## Chapter Two

## Learn About

- AC-130H features
- Locating targets
- AC-130H protection systems

# Inside the AC-130H

The AC-130H is a large, sturdy aircraft. It is nearly 98 feet (30 meters) long and more than 38 feet (11 meters) tall. The distance between its wingtips is about 132 feet (40 meters). This large wingspan helps the aircraft quickly land and take off. The size of the AC-130H allows it to carry weapons and a large crew. It can weigh up to 155,000 pounds (69,750 kilograms) when fully loaded with weapons and equipment.

## Protection

AC-130H pilots often fly low and slow over targets. This practice allows the crew to protect soldiers and attack targets. But flying slowly over targets is dangerous. Enemy troops can easily shoot down slow, low-flying planes. The AC-130H has strong metal plates called armor. The armor protects important parts of the plane from enemy weapons.

The AC-130H also has protection from heat-seeking enemy missiles. A heat-seeking missile has a sensor in its nose. The sensor guides the missile toward a plane's exhaust heat. The AC-130H has exhaust coverings to spread out and cool down the exhaust heat.

AC-130H crew members also can release hot, bright objects called flares to protect the plane from heat-seeking missiles. The missiles may follow the flares instead of the plane.

The AC-130H crew can use a radar jammer to prevent radar-guided missiles from hitting the aircraft. The jammer sends out powerful

**The AC-130H crew sometimes releases flares.**

electronic signals that prevent enemy radar from working properly.

The AC-130H crew also can drop small metal strips called chaff. Each metal strip reflects energy to the radar station. The radar system then has difficulty locating the plane.

## Engines

The AC-130H has four large turboprop engines. Each turboprop engine has a jet engine and a set of metal blades called a propeller. The jet engine turns the propeller. The turning propeller then produces thrust. This force pushes the aircraft through the air.

The engines give the AC-130H a top speed of about 300 miles (500 kilometers) per hour. Many of the Air Force's other planes can travel faster than the AC-130H. The AC-130H must fly slowly to perform close air support and protection missions.

## Night Vision Equipment

Crew members fly the AC-130H mainly at night. The aircraft has a forward-looking infrared (FLIR) system that helps pilots see targets and surroundings. The FLIR system detects heat in objects in the air and on the ground. The location of the objects is displayed on a cockpit screen.

The AC-130H also has a radar system to help crew members locate targets on the ground at night. A second radar system detects signals from

## AC-130H Specifications

| | |
|---|---|
| Function: | Close air support, air interdiction, and force protection |
| Manufacturer: | Lockheed-Martin |
| Date Deployed: | 1972 |
| Length: | 97 feet, 9 inches (29.8 meters) |
| Wingspan: | 132 feet, 7 inches (40.4 meters) |
| Height: | 38 feet, 6 inches (11.7 meters) |
| Weight: | 155,000 pounds (69,750 kilograms) |
| Engine: | Four Allison turboprop engines |
| Speed: | 300 miles (480 kilometers) per hour |
| Range: | 1,500 miles (2,400 kilometers); unlimited with in-flight refueling |
| Crew: | 14 |

electronic sensors on the ground. These sensors can find the movement and location of enemy soldiers and vehicles.

The ASQ-145A Low-Level Light Television (LLLTV) system gathers light from all available sources. It can detect light that is hard for people to see. The ASQ-145A uses the light to locate objects.

### AC-130H Crew

Each AC-130H has 14 crew members. Nine crew members operate sensors or are part of the weapons crew. Sensor operators use equipment to locate targets. Weapons crew members reload the guns and make sure they are ready to be fired.

The other five crew members include the pilot, copilot, navigator, fire control officer, and electronic warfare officer. The navigator helps the two pilots locate targets. The fire control officer makes sure the aircraft's weapons work properly. The electronic warfare officer protects the plane from enemy weapons.

Crew members load a cannon on an AC-130 model.

fuel tank

radar system

# The AC-130H Spectre

propeller

cockpit

105-mm cannon

FLIR sensor

## Chapter Three

## Learn About

- Cannons
- Fire control system
- AC-130H attack method

# Weapons and Tactics

The first Air Force gunships had only short-range machine guns. Pilots needed to fly very low to use them. Enemy ground forces could easily shoot down the gunships.

The AC-130H has two cannons that fire large bullets called shells. The cannons are more powerful and have a longer range than machine guns.

The AC-130H's cannons are powerful.

## Types of Cannons

The AC-130H carries a 40-millimeter (mm) and a 105-mm cannon. The 105-mm cannon can fire larger shells than the 40-mm can. AC-130H crew members often use the 40-mm cannon against enemy soldiers and vehicles. They often use the 105-mm cannon against tanks and underground enemy hideouts called bunkers.

The crew loads the 40-mm cannon with shells. The cannon can fire 100 shells per minute. It may fire armor-piercing shells. These shells have a pointed end designed to pierce armor.

The AC-130H carries 100 shells for the 105-millimeter cannon. Crew members load each shell into the cannon. It can fire six to 10 shells per minute.

The AC-130H's cannons have an accurate fire control system. This system automatically aims the AC-130H's cannons. It often helps crew members hit targets with the first fired shell.

## Tactics

Many types of aircraft can only fire weapons when they are facing targets. Forward-firing planes must turn around to make a second or third attack on a ground target. Enemy soldiers can hide or move before the next attack.

The AC-130H flies in a circle to attack ground targets. Its cannons are on the left side. A circular attack pattern allows the cannons to continuously hit targets.

On protection missions, the AC-130H crew may not fire its weapons. Instead, the presence of the gunship warns enemy forces. The crew flies near the soldiers, buildings, or resources the military wants to protect. The crew members are ready to fire the cannons if needed.

Gunships have good attack and protection systems.

## Chapter Four

## Learn About

AC-130H improvements

The AC-130U

Future AC-130 plans

# The Future

The AC-130H has been an important part of the Air Force for nearly 30 years. AC-130H crew members have participated in several military operations. In 1996, AC-130H crews took part in Operation Assured Response. This operation helped Americans leave the country of Liberia. Fighting had broken out in the African country.

In 2001, AC-130H crews performed missions in Operation Enduring Freedom. This operation targeted terrorists in the Middle Eastern country of Afghanistan.

**The Air Force began to fly the AC-130U in 1994.**

## Improvements

The Air Force has improved the AC-130H throughout its service life. It has updated the AC-130H's FLIR, radar, and fire control systems. The cannon mounts also were redesigned to make them lighter.

In the early 1990s, the Air Force added a Global Positioning System (GPS) to the AC-130H. The GPS helps crew members keep track of their location.

## The AC-130U

In 1994, the Air Force began to fly the AC-130U Spooky. This plane is a replacement for the AC-130A. Aircraft manufacturer Boeing built 13 AC-130Us for the Air Force.

The AC-130U has one of the most advanced aircraft weapon systems in the world. Sensors in the AC-130U's fire control system can aim at two different targets at the same time. The two targets can be up to .6 mile (1 kilometer) away from each other. No other ground attack plane in the world has this ability.

In 2001, military officials announced plans to update and possibly replace the AC-130 gunship models. The new gunship would have advanced sensors and weapons.

Both AC-130Hs and AC-130Us may be replaced in the future. Crews will continue to fly them on missions throughout the world until they become outdated.

# Words to Know

**armor** (AR-mur)—a protective covering

**bunker** (BUHNGK-ur)—an underground shelter from bomb attacks and gunfire

**chaff** (CHAF)—strips of metal foil dropped by an aircraft to confuse enemy radar

**exhaust** (eg-ZAWST)—heated air leaving a jet engine

**propeller** (pruh-PEL-ur)—a set of rotating blades that provides force to move an aircraft through the air

**radar** (RAY-dar)—equipment that uses radio waves to locate and guide objects

**sensor** (SEN-sur)—an instrument that detects physical changes in the environment

**shell** (SHEL)—a large bullet fired from a cannon

**thrust** (THRUHST)—the force created by a jet engine; thrust pushes an airplane forward.

# To Learn More

**Boraas, Tracey.** *U.S. Air Force Special Forces: Special Operations Wings.* Warfare and Weapons. Mankato, Minn.: Capstone Press, 2000.

**Fitzpatrick, Kevin J.** *Flying Gunship: The AC-130 Spectre.* High-Tech Military Weapons. New York: Children's Press, 2000.

**Sievert, Terri.** *The U.S. Air Force at War.* On the Front Lines. Mankato, Minn.: Capstone Press, 2002.

# Useful Addresses

**Air Force Special Operations Command**
Public Affairs Office
229 Cody Avenue, Suite 103
Hurlburt Field, FL  32544-5312

**U.S. Air Force Museum**
110 Spaatz Street
Wright-Patterson AFB, OH  45433

# Internet Sites

Track down many sites about AC-130H Spectres.
Visit the FACT HOUND at *http://www.facthound.com*

## IT IS EASY!  IT IS FUN!

1) Go to *http://www.facthound.com*
2) Type in: 0736815090
3) Click on "FETCH IT" and FACT HOUND will find several links hand-picked by our editors.

**Relax and let our pal FACT HOUND do the research for you!**

# Index